MORE THAN JUST SEX:

IT'S THE ART OF THE CHASE

African American Women Defining Themselves,

Black Men, Each Other, Relationships and Secrets

To Love and Happiness

Gisele Haralson

Published by BookLocker.com, Inc., Bradenton, Florida.

Printed in the United States of America on acid-free paper.

BookLocker.com, Inc.
2015

Second Edition

Disclaimer

This book details the author's personal experiences with and opinions about life and relationships.

The author and publisher are providing this book and its contents on an "as is" basis and make no representations or warranties of any kind with respect to this book or its contents.

Except as specifically stated in this book, neither the author or publisher, nor any authors, contributors, or other representatives will be liable for damages arising out of or in connection with the use of this book. This is a comprehensive limitation of liability that applies to all damages of any kind, including (without limitation) compensatory; direct, indirect or consequential damages; loss of data, income or profit; loss of or damage to property and claims of third parties.

This book provides content related to life and relationship topics. As such, use of this book implies your acceptance of this disclaimer.

Acknowledgments

I must first thank God from whom all my blessings truly come. I would like to extend my deepest thanks and appreciation to all the sisters who allowed me into their lives and shared their stories and advice with me. It was a wonderful journey filled with laughter and sorrow. I also would like to thank my mother for always being my number one fan and supporting me in whatever endeavors I embrace. My friends and family have been a tremendous source of support during this very difficult year and I love them all for their prayers, words of comfort, and encouragement. There is no other relationship like that of sisters, and my sister and I have always been very close. I want to take this opportunity to extend my heartfelt appreciation and love to her for all she has done to lift my spirits during moments of despair and discouragement as I learn to live life without my rock, my best friend, Joseph Haralson and move on with life without my anchor. My husband was the cherry on top of my cake; he had always been there for me, and the love we shared was the most meaningful aspect of my life.

Table of Contents

Introduction

The last two and a half years have been among the most difficult, transforming, and enlightening years of my life. The completion of my graduate studies, the diagnosis of my husband with cancer, and his ultimate death all catapulted me into a world of pain, growth, and discovery. The success of *More Than Just Sex: It's The Art of the Chase - African American Women Defining Themselves, Black Men, Each Other, Relationships, and Secrets to Love, and Happiness,* was a result of encouragement from many friends and loved ones.

It was around the end of my first year in graduate school while I was attending church services with my husband that the priest distributed a publication and referred to an article entitled "Why Don't African Americans Marry?", which really struck a chord with me. The article revealed that black women in their twenties and early thirties wanted to marry and commit to a relationship at a time when black men their age are more likely to enjoy playing the field. The article also referenced a piece in the Washington Post entitled "Marriage Is for White People: The Decline of Marriage Among African Americans." The article was written by an author who was teaching a career exploration class to a group of sixth graders, when a young African American boy revealed that he thought that marriage was only for white people. It was at that moment that I knew that I wanted to research how sisters felt about marriage and relationships within the African American community and what would make a young boy come up with such a thought.

As I would talk to sisters about this topic, they were blown away and always seemed to have some interesting stories to share. I was really surprised by their overwhelming interest and desire to share their perceptions and attitudes on the institution of marriage and relationships.

With a great support base, I immediately pulled together a focus group of sisters who were married, single, divorced, widowed, and cohabiting to allow them to openly express their feelings. Over wine and hors d'oeuvres, we really dug into some of the issues that sisters face within marriage, their quest to get married, as well as finding the ideal partner.

Statistics show that African American women are less likely to marry, less likely to stay married, and less likely to remarry after their marriage ends. With this in mind; the book provides sisters with a place to reveal their concerns, pains, joys, hopes, and fears regarding marriage and relationships they have experienced and what they have learned and continue to learn.

It is my goal for sisters to use this book, not as a guide for relationships but as a means to share views and lessons learned. I hope that the information shared will really move sisters to the point of realization and self-improvement. Some sisters often use finance, status, looks, and other barriers to keep themselves from finding true love or staying in bad relationships. This book will reveal and explore how sisters sometimes miss out on love because of mistakes, insecurities, and bad relationship choices.

I have spent the last eight years motivating and assisting African American women to become self- sufficient and strive for greatness. During these years, I have had the privilege of getting to know many sisters, and found myself quite concerned and shocked by the continual problems and issues they seemed to be experiencing within their relationships. Now, let me say that I've made a few bad choices myself, but I'm happy to say that I not only survived the painful journey, but I use these experiences as learning opportunities.

I have attempted to address issues that are indigenous to the African American community. I have collected facts directly from sisters; their names have been changed to assure anonymity, and their stories are true. They have articulated their truths, discussed how they felt, and were able to think through their real feelings about relationships and their personal lives with other sisters. Life is a continual chase; we spend our lives in pursuit of many things, the ultimate being love and happiness. I hope this book will be as informative, enjoyable, and therapeutic to you as it was for me while writing it.

Chapter 1

Defining and Evaluating You

Selecting a companion to share your life with is an important decision, probably one of the most important decisions you will ever have to make. Knowing this, your mission should be to establish a pleasant and pleasing relationship. In order for women to do this, it is critical that they become comfortable with themselves. Many sisters get involved in relationships as a means of filling a void in their lives. They begin seeing brothers as their source of happiness. What sisters are saying is, "I need you to complete me or to make me whole." In dialoguing with numerous women during the last three years, the most common mistake I observed is that some women neglect to take inventory of themselves, including their liabilities, as well as what they can offer a mate in a relationship. A healthy relationship needs to be balanced, and they need to know that just as they are looking for the ideal man, he is also looking for the ideal woman. All the men in the world cannot make a woman happy if she is not happy with herself.

My advice to any woman is to take a good look at her life, look within her soul, and be truthful and realize that contrary to what she may have been told, brothers admire and like a strong, confident woman. There is something that is special when brothers see their lady accomplish great things and become successful through her own work. A sister must feel good about who she is and work on becoming the best person she can be.

I think that every woman should ask herself questions like "Am I satisfied with the direction my life is going? Why should

Mr. Right choose me?" These questions could help a sister evaluate where she is before embarking on a relationship with the mindset that her happiness depends upon what someone else does or fails to do.

COMMENTS:

I define myself as a unique individual that God has designed to do those special tasks that were designated for me only. I am a strong individual who has overcome many obstacles in my life but have not allowed any of them to keep me down. I take all challenges head-on. When fighting battles that I sometimes do not understand, I make sure my whole armor of God is on, and I stand my ground, giving it all that I have. I am one of determination, self-confidence, intelligence, and honesty.

----- *Monique*

My commitment to my family and my faith define who I am. Integrity is important to me. I am honest. I love my family. I do my best to serve underserved families around me. I want to make sure my family is community-conscious and gives back to the community, like I do. I love my family.

----- *Gina*

I would define myself as a person who is currently looking for betterment. What I mean by that is that I'm striving to become a well-rounded individual. I'm striving to attain more from an educational and work perspective. I'm striving to find my purpose in life and attain it. And I want nothing more than to have a closer relationship with God. I believe that I'm a pretty honest person. I have high moral and ethical beliefs that only allow me to do what I think is right. I think I am an easygoing person, but I try not to let people misuse me or mistake that for weakness.

------ *Jordan*

My morals and values define who I am. They define how I conduct myself from day to day. I am sincere, considerate, kind, and a very sensitive woman who loves God, family, and friends.

------*Mia*

I am strong, polite, caring, and intelligent, but a very sensitive woman. I'm a very complex person with a lot of views with which the majority of people don't always agree.

----- *Nicole*

I am giving, empathetic, a defender of those I perceive as helpless, and emotional.

-----*Dana*

I am not defined by what I own or how I look. I am defined by the positive feelings I have inside me and by the love I feel for myself, my GOD, and others, not necessarily in that order. I think positively of myself. I never stop trying to improve and redefine myself.

----- *Anita*

I define myself as an educated, strong black woman who loves God, my daughter, and myself. I love life and cherish each and every day to the fullest. I am a giving and thoughtful person.

-----*Wanda*

I am defined by beliefs, character, and actions. I am an African-American woman who is strong, independent, and driven but yet vulnerable, sensitive, and at times...alone (even though I'm married).

------*Veronica*

GH Final Thoughts:

Here you see sisters having a clear understanding of who they are and how God and faith has shaped them into the individuals they are. Anita talks about loving who she is and constantly trying to improve herself. As you can see, the common denominator with these sisters is that they all seem to be confident, caring, and well-rounded individuals who have a strong sense of self. The secret to captivating the interest of brothers is to realize that you must bring as much to the relationship as he does, which includes your ideas, interests, hobbies, and thought. Many sisters are often trying to portray or define themselves through the lens of what they think their partner wants to see.

Veronica describes herself as strong, independent, driven, but yet vulnerable, sensitive, and at times lonely, even though she is married. Often sisters have the idea that a man will fill all empty areas in their lives, but even a husband can't always fill all areas all the time, and you have to learn to look within you and to God for fulfillment and inner peace. Don't ever try to change yourself for anyone, but always strive to improve yourself for you.

Chapter 2

You Are Going to Love Me

So many times sisters spend a considerable amount of time and energy trying to do everything in their power to make brothers love and be with them, even if these brothers have given all the telltale signs that they are not ready to settle down. It has always been my philosophy that you cannot make anyone do anything he/she does not want to do. I think everyone has heard the old saying, "You can lead a horse to water, but you can't make him drink." Until sisters realize that they cannot continue to close their eyes to the behaviors of brothers who are saying, "I am not interested in a committed relationship with you," they will forever keep setting themselves up for pain and heartache. Then sisters begin blaming brothers because they will not do what they want them to do.

All too often, sisters develop feelings of frustration and anger, and they begin dwelling on the negative characterization of brothers. This tends to create a vicious cycle of negativity that permeates relationships. With this in mind, I was reminded of a conversation I had over lunch with an associate who shared a story about a friend of hers who was involved in a long-distance relationship with a man from her hometown. The couple had attended college together. Upon graduating, her boyfriend landed a job in their hometown, while she became employed at the university. This sister, holding a highly professional job, loaned her boyfriend $3,000 for some expenses he had incurred. OK, this might not be that big of a deal, depending on whom you ask, but when her boyfriend decided to visit the city in which she lived, he did not find it necessary to let her know that he would be in town and made every effort possible to keep her from knowing that he was visiting. But once she discovered he was there and staying with one of his college friends, he still refused to spend any quality time with her, opting to hang out with his boys. Now, to add insult to injury, when this young sister planned a trip to her hometown, which is where her boyfriend lives, it was she who insisted that she stay with him during her visit in order to spend some quality time with him. Although he did not reject her offer, he would not take her out and wanted to stay at home the entire time. I don't know whether I am crazy or not, but something doesn't seem to be right with this picture, and what is more amazing to me is that this sister actually is convinced that this guy is her man.

During my research for this book, I had many wonderful opportunities to meet and talk to many brothers and sisters to get an understanding of where their heads were. And depending upon whom you asked and where they were in their relationships, I heard many viewpoints about this situation and how this young lady should handle this situation.

It would be wise for sisters to understand the persistent and manipulative ploys by brothers that are intended only to get them in bed. There are a large number of brothers whose sole purpose in pursuing a relationship with a sister is sexual. A good relationship does not develop as a result of a sexual experience. Sisters should have the awareness necessary to recognize that infidelity and the inability to be monogamous is a trait that some men possess.

It is my view that one of the major reasons some sisters are experiencing unhealthy relationships is that some are bypassing loving and nurturing men for the pretentious, smooth-talking, good-for-nothing playboys who are often in a relationship with at least two or three other women. It has always puzzled me as to why some sisters would rather live with an unpredictable and challenging man whose mission in the relationship seems to be to keep sister's heads hurting. But what amazed me more than anything else is how they aggressively battle with the brothers as well as other sisters with whom they know he is in a relationship and literally stress themselves out for a brother who is often using them until they can find the woman who can meet their desire. Please allow me to say this: If you don't know that he is in a relationship with someone else, that is one thing, but when you know there are other women in his life, you are opening yourself up to unnecessary pain and suffering.

There are some women who seem to be so desperate for a man that they will settle for any man, which is really sad. If you allow brothers to treat you in a less than desirable way or to disrespect you, then you cannot get upset when they do what you have allowed them to do. I think what a lot of sisters might not know is that a bad relationship is worse than no relationship.

COMMENTS:

> African American females, in my opinion, possess some negative aspects. Their lack of self-respect and respect from their men and no hard work ethics of bygone days are missing. By the same token, hope still exists for change.
>
> -----*Shelia*

> A large percentage of women commit too early in a relationship, before a man wants to be monogamous. We like him and then we dream of "walking down the aisle with him." He, on the other hand, only wants to date us because he wants to get to know us (he has

other ulterior motives as well). We need to learn to be friends and control the urge to take it to the next level before the man is ready.

-----Jessica

African American women often give up a lot and suppress their true desires in order to keep peace, keep relationships with males, and keep family together. For this reason we carry a lot of responsibilities and burdens unnecessarily, and most of the burdens are self-inflicted. When we don't operate in this manner, we are considered a threat, disrespectful, and out of line by the African American male.

-----Raven

GH Final Thoughts:

Holding out on sex seems to be one of the hardest things for some women. Whatever happened to making a brother work for it? I don't know whether there is this feeling that the sex you are giving is the best he has ever had, or your skills far outweigh the skills of the other females with whom he may be currently having sex. Maybe you think that once you are done with him he will be so mesmerized that no other woman will stand a chance. But whatever the mind-set may be, sisters must realize that relationships are not built on sex. This is the message that Jessica is addressing when she talks about moving too fast and not taking time to develop a friendship before engaging in sex, which for many women could lead to an emotional connection which may not be shared. If you noticed, she pointed out how quickly sisters begin dreaming about walking down the aisle only to later discover that the feelings are not mutual, which can be very painful. Understand that there is something much more than sex that makes a brother stay in a relationship. It is that magnetic feeling that you put into his heart which makes him feel like he is on top of the world and nothing else matters but you and him.

Chapter 3

Stuck on Money, Stuck on Status

Sociological studies support the theory that while black men choose women by their degree of attractiveness, black women choose men by their degree of status. Many black women dream of meeting and marrying a man with money. But for the majority of black women, the reality of this is probably just that, "a dream." The fact is that black women now earn nearly two thirds of all bachelor's and master's degrees that are awarded to African Americans as well as achieve occupational status and positions that carry prestige. With this in mind, many sisters who have made it professionally are looking for brothers with prestige, status, and money. Many of these sisters have had to work very hard and made lots of sacrifices to get to where they are, and they feel they deserve a brother who has done the same.

Now, I can understand a sister feeling this way, but the reality is although there are good and eligible brothers out there, the truth is that professional black women greatly outnumber professional black men. There are simply not enough of these kinds of black men to go around, and this relentless quest of finding brothers with big money and status has led many sisters to a life of loneliness and unhappiness. In my opinion, too many sisters are judging brothers solely on what kind of work they are doing or what kind of car they are driving. This is a big mistake! What is actually happening is some sisters are overlooking good blue collar working brothers who are sometimes making twice as much money as some white collar workers, thus denying themselves an opportunity of possibly finding true love.

Let me say this, before going on. I am not saying for sisters to overlook professional brothers and just set their sights on blue collar men only. That is not what I am saying, but you have to be realistic and aware of what is going on within the dating game. First, there are some well-to-do brothers out there, and not all of them are rappers, playing sports, or entertainers, but let's face it, the competition for these brothers is great. The really rich brothers are often looking for trophy wives to add glamour to their impressive lifestyles. Usually these brothers are often interested in women who are extremely beautiful, possess great talent or fame, are a part of the Black elite, or are White. For the record, not all brothers go this route, but I must admit, a lot of them do. It is really nice to see brothers who make the decision to stay with the sisters who were with them before the money.

This falls in line with what a good friend of mine shared with a group about a conversation she had with her pastor before getting married. She said, "This could be where some black women miss out" She continued by saying, "We all have a vision; who doesn't want to have a man that has money? Everybody wants to have the money. But usually that's not how it goes; usually we live in a society where you need two salaries." But what her pastor had said was that this could be where sisters miss out sometimes on a great guy who has a good blue collar job, and we overlook them. Here is where she hit the bull's-eye, saying, "The main focus in regards to finances or money is that if the brother has a vision or a goal, then you have something to work with, but if he doesn't have a vision, or doesn't have a goal for his life, then you have a problem." She concluded by stating, "Sure, a guy should have a job when he gets married. Maybe he doesn't have the kind of job you would like for him to have; maybe he is not making the amount of money you would like for him to make, but if you all work out a plan and he has a vision for greater things, then that shouldn't be minimized."

I totally agree with this sister, and realize that everyone doesn't always get to the top at the same pace. I was in my late twenties before I received my first degree, which was great for me because until that time I was not serious about school. But once I made up my mind about the direction I wanted my life to go, I knew what needed to be done to make it happen.

I am fully aware of the importance of being supportive of your partner's dreams, but I also understand how some sisters feel when they have assisted and aided a brother in his vision and the dream doesn't quite turn out the way they had planned. One thing that we all know is that life has no guarantees. We all take chances; sometimes we win, and sometimes we lose. This topic of discussion prompted a huge debate among the group. After listening to this intense exchange, one sister countered with her reservations about supporting some brother's visions. Her concern was this idea of your mate having a vision which may or may not include you. She proceeded by saying, "You might have initially been a part of his vision, but after the money and success begins; he gradually eliminates you from the vision." That is why she refuses to depend upon any man for money; she always believed in having her own money and realized that it is important that relationships are built on a strong and solid foundation, not on material possessions.

So what you have going on is brothers and sisters at odds with each other. Sisters are saying that brothers select mates based on looks, or the way women are shaped. Brothers, on the other hand, claim that sisters choose mates based on money and how much they have. As a sociologist who has studied relationships, I know this is very true, but the message that must be transmitted to brothers and sisters is that it really isn't about how much money a man has or how fine a sister is or how good she looks; the real concern is the connection you and he feel with each other and the trust that must be present if any relationship is expected to move forward in a productive and positive way. So my question is:

Are sisters looking for a good man or fat pockets?

I am sure everyone has heard sisters griping about the fact that there are no good men available. But the questions I immediately ask is where are you looking for these men and what do you consider a good man? Are you truly looking for a good, hardworking man, or are you looking for someone from whom to milk money? It is certainly no secret that, a lot of women are looking for a man to take care of them. As I have said before, I believe that there is nothing wrong with wanting to have someone to do nice things for you, but it should go both ways. A good relationship is built on give and take. So many sisters, despite their own accomplishments, feel that they must catch a brother with fat pockets, often with little or no regard for how he is making the money. I think you know where I am going here. These women are setting themselves up for a terrible misfortune.

There is absolutely nothing wrong with having some of the finer things in life and being pampered. I am a true believer that sisters should be pampered and treated to the best. But what I do find disturbing is sisters selling themselves to the highest bidder, and what often comes along with the deal are sisters not being respected and treated with no dignity. What gradually happens is that they become controlled and weakened by money. Women like this will use their bodies to entrap a man in exchange for things. As time passes on, they may begin to believe the man is falling in love with them. Then, when the brother makes her aware that the relationship was nothing more than sexual, she is often hurt and disappointed. Of course, you know a sister wants to know.

Does his money and his status equal happiness?
There is this big misconception that social status and money equal happiness. There is nothing farther from the truth. In fact, some research shows that the divorce rates are higher among high-status African American men. It is my opinion that some successful, educated, middle-class brothers consider themselves as "the catch" are using this as an avenue to sleep with as many women as heavenly possible that will allow them. But this is where sisters often get the game twisted. They think if they are hooking up with a brother of high social standing and money, their relationship comes with a guarantee of instant happiness. That is what we have been conditioned to think. Money, power, status, and prestige bring great happiness. But as a friend of mine who played an influential role in my writing this book expressed in regard to having a brother with big money. She firmly talked about not caring if a brother had a million dollars in his account, because as she so bluntly put it, "What good is money when you are with someone who is controlling, closed minded, selfish, and has no morals or values?"

I am sure everyone has heard the old saying, that not everything that shines is gold. The people in magazines and on the movie screens make it look so easy-- riding around town in their luxury cars, spending their husband's money, vacationing in the south of France-- all give the illusion that their lives are filled with joy. What a life, but let me let you in on a little secret-- relationships take work, and there are no guarantees.

COMMENTS:

Having financial stability is very important when it comes to finding a mate. Love and respect are challenged by lack of financial stability. Some relationships suffer because partners are not honest with each other about the importance of a steady and stable income. It is a shared responsibility and should be planned and agreed on. Lack of financial stability can lead to resentment and negative feelings in a relationship.

-----*Trisha*

It is extremely important to me that a brother have a college degree. Both my grandmothers have college degrees. When I graduated from high school, the question was not *whether* I was going to college but *where* I was going to college. I desire a mate who believes a college degree is equally important so we can instill the same value in our children and grandchildren.

-----*Tonya*

Money does not make a relationship better, but it does make it easier when it's not an issue. In any relationship, finances will cause it to fail if there is not enough there, or is not budgeted correctly. It's important to make sure that in a relationship, certainly before marriage, that discussions have taken place about who will handle the checkbook and what will the monthly budget be in the household.

-----Monique

Financial stability is extremely important. Two people together should not be financially worse off than one of the parties before the union.

----Dana

Financial stability is also important in the scheme of things, but there again GOD, love, and honor are more important.

-----Shelia

Education is important when I become involved with someone; however, all people with an education doesn't make them a better person than someone without an education. I want my mate to be knowledgeable, intelligent, and willing to be open to learning new things. He must be able to maintain employment, pay his bills, and know how to budget. Also have a vision for our future, investments, opening a business, etc. This is important to know how he will handle our household in the future.

-----Dawn

A lot of sisters are dependent. I am not talking about all women, but a lot of women depend on men for happiness and finances. Get out and find yourself a job and work to take care of yourself and your children, if you have any.

------*Nicole*

Financial stability is very important. I don't need any help to spend my salary. The addition of a mate should increase your earnings or allow you to save more money or make more investments.

------*Shonda*

Having a degree is not as important as a brother following his dreams and with those dreams, having financial independence. As long as he is able to support the household and there aren't any hang-ups, the relationship should survive. I would rather you own your own company without a degree, than have a degree and not have a job.

------*Toi*

The younger sisters, I feel are "get overs."
However, my perception is changing because many are
beginning to do things for themselves.

-----*Tasha*

I believe the importance of education depends on
the individual. I think that mates/spouses should be in
sync with each other according to the things they have in
common. That's what's important. If one person is more
educated than the other, this can cause the couple to be
very unequal in more ways than one. I think it's
important for couples to find common elements between
each other, and education does not have to be the
answer.

-----*Brianna*

I believe financial stability depends on the
individual. Each person should be financially stable
within themselves. That way no one person is dependent
on the other. This causes less confusion in a
relationship.

-----*Jordan*

GH Final Thoughts:

These sisters each feel strongly that financial stability is very important in a relationship. Financial issues are among the leading causes of divorce in the United States, and given the fact that African American males earn substantially less than white males, one can understand the pressure on a brother who has the desire to provide for his family but feels that the burdens and inequities seem too great to bear.

When one person (it could be a brother or a sister) has to carry the entire load of a household on his or her back, it could lead to resentment and negative feelings which could cause tension within the relationship, as Trisha stated. In my opinion, brothers and sisters both should contribute financially, given the fact that in the average American household it takes two incomes to make ends meet. With this said, I am aware that there are some brothers who are making enough money to allow their wives to stay at home and live a life of leisure or take on that very important job of raising their children, and if this is your case then, go for it!! But the only advice I would give sisters would be to make sure to think about a few things before taking on this position. First, if you noticed, I did say wives, not girlfriends or babies' mama; that word "WIFE" could come with benefits. It is my hope that a sister would not just put her life on hold and think that a brother is going to stay content with giving her money for her every need. Secondly, it is wise for sisters to have some kind of educational background, vocational training, or credentials, like, an associate, bachelor, or master's degree, etc…. Finally, they need to have some kind of work experience. Sisters need to know what it feels like to have been in the work force just in case they find themselves separated or divorced and having to take care of themselves again.

It has been proven that after a divorce or separation, women and their children often struggle financially. Single-parent family structures are frequently accompanied by conditions of economic instability and high poverty rates. As stated in chapter 8, of all major demographic groups, African American single-mothers and their children are the worst off economically. Given this information, it is imperative that sisters are vigilant in regard to their financial well-being. Nicole and Tasha both feel that some sisters need to stop trying to use brothers and start paving their own way in life. There is nothing worse than a sister being in a position of not being able to support herself and feeling that every man that she comes across is obligated to provide for her.

Although Tasha felt that some sisters are "get overs" she has come to discover that more are beginning to understand the importance of taking care of themselves. My observation is that very few brothers these days are willing to support a sister who is not bringing anything to the table. Then, of course, there are also a number of brothers who are looking for sisters to take care of them. Believe me when I say life can be so much better if a sister and her man both have social status, education, and money. There is nothing like a sister having her own financial independence and understanding that in order to enjoy a higher quality of life she and her partner need to be productive members of society, which will enhance, enrich, and increase their fulfillment in life.

Chapter 4

Sisterly Advice

I am an idealist who advocates for sisters taking care of themselves and living the American Dream. I also believe if you work very hard, believe in yourself, and trust in God, there is nothing you cannot achieve, including happiness.

It was my godmother who really gave some advice regarding marriage that I thought was absolutely phenomenal; she communicated to a group that, "Not every day is going to be peaches and cream. You are going to have arguments about simple things like food. You have to make sensible decisions; it is just a meal." She said, "Never go to bed mad at your mate, and never let him walk out the door mad at you; it can be a terrible thing, you might not see him again." She shared a story about a friend of hers who had an argument with her husband. Before leaving, he tried to kiss her, and she pushed him away; the next news she received at her job was that her husband had been killed in a car accident. To me personally, there is no greater pain than losing someone you love, but under those conditions it must have been horrifying. My godmother also urged the group, "Try to iron out your grievances, so you can rest, and if he goes out and something would happen- praise God, you never want it to happen- you don't have that on your conscience that you were mad about something." Finally, she went on to say, "You should not feel bad in saying you are sorry, forgive me, I'm sorry, I didn't mean to hurt your feelings; bend your pride, you got to work it out."

This piece of advice really stuck with me in a way I didn't realize until my husband was diagnosed with cancer. It was at that moment that I could really see the big picture; I began to understand that it is not always about who is right or who is wrong, but being able to love your partner, despite of their shortcomings, and really understanding that no one is perfect, not even you.

COMMENTS:

My first advice would be to put God first in any decision that you make, and there you cannot go wrong. But you also have to make sure that the decisions that you've made when it comes to your relationship, family, and career complete you. You shouldn't settle for anything. Make sure the total package is there when it comes to supporting your happiness and your drive for life. Your decisions should make you want to live and be excited about living.

------*Monique*

You can have it all, as long as you have a committed partner and you balance the aspects of your life that are important to you. It will take both of you to decide how to define the balance.

-----*Jessica*

Seek a relationship with God. Not only will He reveal your purpose, but he will also help you plan the action for your relationships, careers, and family, etc.

-----Mia

My advice is for both African American men and women when it comes to relationships, family, and careers. Prioritize and decide on what you want to fully commit. Contrary to some, you cannot do it all (successfully) simultaneously. At some point, something will be placed on the back burner. It's all about balance and compromise. You never accomplish something by yourself. There is always someone who has helped contribute to your success. Make sure you openly communicate with the people you rely on for support and consider what they may be giving up to ensure your success.

-----Kim

Women tend to give more than they receive. Therefore, if a man can love you for you, then you're on the right path. Anything you give to GOD and let HIM work out cannot fail.

-----Anita

I would tell all African American females to put God first, trust him to send the mate he has prepared for you. I would also stress to them that sex is overrated and you can't miss something you never had, so wait! Wait, I say, on the Lord and be of good courage for he will give you the desires of your heart.

-----*Dawn*

Be true to yourself. After God, love yourself first. When possible, take care of you, but do so with balance. Find that balance with yourself, your relationship, career, and family. You will know when it is out of balance when you are not at peace within and when there is external struggle. Also, learn how to communicate honestly, effectively, and with love. Speak facts, not always feelings, and don't hesitate to forgive (let go) or admit when you make a mistake. Be flexible, but without losing yourself.

------*Brianna*

Stay in school; don't let yourself go; don't depend on anyone; and no one owes you anything.

------*Tonya*

The advice that I would give to an African American woman when it comes to a relationship is that there's nothing wrong with having or setting expectations, but be ready to compromise. Let her know that things won't always go the way she may plan.

Family comes first, but her husband is the head of her household......anyone else is second in line. There's nothing wrong with having a career, but she should realize that she has to still put her husband and family before that. That's according to the Bible.

----Yolanda

If you are married, GOD needs to be in the relationship, and you should respect your husband as the head of his house. But whether you are married or not, don't feel that a man validates who you are. With relationships, it's a give and take and a lot of compromise. There's no room for anyone being selfish. As a wife and mother, you should be there to take care of your home, husband, and children. I also feel that a woman can have it all, family, relationship, and career, but everything needs to have a balance. If you feel overwhelmed with all of this, communication should be used.

-----Rena

African American women should know and accept their role within their family. Respect yourself before you demand respect from others. Excel in your career, yet your family should be priority number one. Stop being so aggressive with males! Allow yourself to truly experience courtship. Good, old-fashioned morals and values should form the foundation of your life.

-----Jada

Please! Please! Please! Get to know yourself. If you don't know you, it is not fair to expect or even demand that your partner does. Prioritize your life... what's most important to you now and what you think it will be in the future. Exp: I thought I was the career professional and it was me with my brief case and there was a time that I'd work 12 plus hour days and or bring work home... My husband is an adult, so he could take care of himself and he's not much of a talker (I'd make sure he had dinner) and he worked at night, so I could work all those hours guilt free. Then I became a mother. Even though I'm the mother of only one child, he is my life. I never thought I'd want to trade in my briefcase for a diaper bag, but I did. I never stopped working and didn't change much when he was a baby, but now that he's six, since I still HAVE to work, my work day ends promptly at 5 pm and I try not to bring any work home (I've even been behind because I wouldn't bring it home) because from 5:01pm daily, I am Mommy, and that's the most wonderful feeling for me! That is his time. My point is that 10 years ago, I would have never thought I rather be a "stay at home" mom over a corporate mogul, but I do… My, how things change. Fortunately, until I have my own agency, the one I work for is quite beneficial for me and my family. Don't forget to try to project your goals and objectives for the future.

-----*Veronica*

GH Final Thoughts:

It has always been my mission in life to encourage women, men, and young children to strive for greatness. There is something that is so attractive about a woman giving of herself to improve the lives of others. I am a firm believer there is nothing in life that you can't achieve if you only put your mind and God to it. These sisters have shared their wisdom and advice with you in hopes that you will in turn encourage and inspire other sisters. As African American women, we really should consider reaching out to other sisters in hopes of connecting and motivating.

Chapter 5

What Do Sisters Really Want?

Regardless of race or ethnicity, women in general when asked what they want in a mate, the answer remains the same: to be loved in a relationship of joint empowerment, instead of struggling for control and ongoing conflict. Sisters want someone to listen to them and accept them for who they are. Not only do they want their thoughts and feelings to matter, they want to enjoy an emotional and spiritual connection, not just a sexual one, with their mate. Sisters want sensitive and caring brothers and the opportunity to experience life and the world around them with a man they can trust and love.

Loving relationships between brothers and sisters do not have to consist of a power struggle. A relationship is really about accomplishing the same goals and working together to reach them, which is what many sisters are looking for. Sisters are smart, clever, witty, and would love to be able to share their life with someone who equally shares their mission for happiness and companionship.

Even though many sisters would love to have a man who is ready to make a commitment, there are segments of women who, for whatever reason, choose not to commit to a relationship. I remember my mother saying that she never wanted to marry because of how mean and jealous her father was toward her mother. My mother talked about how afraid she was when her parents would argue; she described feeling that her heart was going to jump out of her chest because it was beating so hard. These fears and experiences were engraved in my mother's mind, and they shaped the course of her life as a single mother and African American women. Although these were my mother's experiences, she never pushed them on me and often reminded me that the vows I took in matrimony were very important.

COMMENTS:

From a relationship, I want a godly man who loves me as God loves the church. I want a man who knows how to treat me like the queen I am and to be loving, kind, patient, giving, responsible, and outgoing. I want him to be my best friend.

------*Dawn*

There is nothing better than being in a loving, committed relationship; that is what I want.

------*Ashley*

I want a lifelong commitment of open communication, loyalty, friendship, laughter, support, lots of hugs, kisses, I Love You, and intimacy.

------*Tasha*

What I want first of all, is someone who loves me as much as I love him; that person needs to give me respect as well. This would not be for the sake of my fulfillment, but because I could accept nothing less.

------*Shelia*

I want honesty, trust, sincerity, open and nonjudgmental communication; a man who has a genuine love for me.

------*Brenda*

In my relationship, I want me and my spouse to adventure to another level in Christ (growing together). I want us to show love towards each other as though there were no tomorrow. And lastly, I want us to be able to communicate with an open heart (without judgment).

------*Jordan*

I want friendship that slowly grows into a mutual love and commitment. I want a man who is committed to me and ready to settle down with me only. Infidelity hurts and creates an unhealthy relationship. It sometimes takes a lifetime to recover from its effects.

------*Trisha*

I want peace from a relationship. Peace is necessary to enjoy and appreciate life to its fullest.

------Dana

Love, communication, and most of all trust is what I want. It's the best feeling when you can be free in every sense of the way with your spouse.

-------Rena

GH Final Thoughts:

There is a natural desire for individuals to want to be loved and cared for by someone. Although some sisters may not want to admit it, bad relationships have led many women to refuse to open up their hearts and emotions to brothers out of fear of being hurt or rejected.

These sisters in this chapter know exactly what they want from a relationship and wasted no time getting right to the point. They talk about godliness, commitment, trust, honesty, mutual love, open communication, friendship, respect, and most of all peace. There is no better feeling than the feeling of peace and happiness. But the key to fulfillment within a relationship is fulfillment of self. I have heard people say the way you start a relationship is often what becomes the foundation; therefore, if you enter a relationship displaying no self- love, demanding no respect, and settling for whatever a brother gives you, then how could you possibly think that your relationship is going to blossom into something beautiful. Love is understanding that not every day will be filled with happiness and joy, but realizing that there is a comfort in knowing that you have a partner that is yours and who loves and respects you for who you are.

Chapter 6

Understanding Black Men

I loved my black man because he first loved me. He was passionate but difficult; loving but stern, it was not until we were able to understand each other that things started to make sense in our relationship. I am so grateful that I was able to experience a remarkable relationship filled with magnificent highs and dreadful lows, but it all made me into a stronger and wiser woman. I have often been asked about my feelings about losing my husband, and the only thing that comes to mind is that there are people who have lived a lifetime and not experienced the love, joy, and passion we showered upon each other. I was so lucky to have had him for the time I did.

I am indeed convinced that a number of brothers travel through life confused and unable to recognize the secret to a loving relationship. I strongly feel that in order for brothers to be able to commit to someone in a long-term monogamous relationship, they must learn to first love themselves.

Just as I stated in a previous chapter, it is critical for women to take a good look at themselves and evaluate; brothers also need to really know themselves and come to terms with their entire being. Once this has been accomplished, brothers should embrace and accept the negative and positive aspects of themselves, which should allow them to develop a true sense of who they really are.

Becoming vulnerable to their own emotions and feelings is not something that brothers have learned to do. Often they have been taught that the number of women they score is a direct indicator of their manhood. The results of this kind of thinking are destructive to a potential relationship. When are our brothers going to realize that sex is not the answer to every good or bad thing that happens within a relationship? I recently talked to a friend who confided that she and her husband had been in conflict for the past week and had not been talking to each other for days. But after seven days had passed, her husband called to see whether she was interested in having sex when he came home from work. In his mind, this was his way of resolving the issues they had been having for the past week.

There will always be conflict between brothers and sisters regarding what they want in a relationship until they are able to learn to communicate with each other (which will be covered in a later chapter). It is important that they both understand that relationships at times can be very difficult for everyone involved, especially children. But for some brothers who tend to resolve and define themselves through sex, it can be downright tragic.

The reason for some of this behavior is that it is not common for black men and women to have grown up in a two-parent home. Many young brothers have never observed how men function in a positive relationship. The examples of male and female interactions are often relationships filled with lies, betrayal, infidelity, permissive behaviors, and abuses. With these behaviors as everyday fixtures in their minds, there is no wonder that some young brothers are finding it difficult to develop loving and supportive relationships.

But it is truly my belief that if these young brothers were taught love and respect for women by seeing their fathers love and respect their mothers, then they would be better equipped with the fundamentals needed to interact within relationships. It is important that brothers open their minds to embracing what a healthy relationship looks like, and in doing this, I have no doubt that brothers will love their partner with all the passion, satisfaction, and excitement that any sister could ever dream of.

COMMENTS:

I understand that the African American men have lost their insight on what their ancestry is all about. They are expected to be strong, but are also expected to be open-minded and sensitive to their mate's needs as a woman. I expect my brothers to take the time to learn how to appreciate the sincere beauty of the African American woman. I understand that you choose to blame others for your faults instead of picking up the torch and keeping the fire lit so that the midnight oil will burn into the early morning so that you won't be an excuse, but instead a living testimony.

-------*Monique*

African American males have a lot of obstacles they have to overcome. I believe that some black males make things in their life more difficult than they have to be, especially when dealing with a mate or spouse. I believe this has everything to do with their upbringing or family orientation.

------*Yolanda*

Honestly, I believe the best example of what the African American male is or should be is found in men over the age of 45 years. Our younger men seem to have lost the desire to succeed, and they settle for far less than they are capable of achieving. Our younger men are accepting of the status quo and often do not strive for more, whether it be financially, socially, or even in relationships (paternal, intimate, or otherwise). There was a time when black men saw an injustice and fought against it, without a gun. There were times when black men believed in providing for their families even if it took 3 jobs while the wife took care of home. I'm not saying women shouldn't help, but I'm saying... Women were held at a higher regard. We accept it when a white woman stays home with the kids when her husband is out working, but if a black woman stays home, she's either lazy or should be helping her man. There was a time when a black man didn't want his woman to have to endure what he did everyday... the indignities, so he did what he had to do to provide for his family, and the women were supportive, not necessarily submissive. There is a difference! Somehow, somewhere along the road, our younger African American males lost that drive. They are driven to "have" things, not to "achieve" things. Our younger men often feel entitled and didn't earn a thing. Take a look back in history at the NBA and those who broke barriers and set records, and compare their salaries to the stars of today; it's staggering. I'm sure they are proud of these young men, but it also must be a sort of a "slap in the face" to see how their money is squandered and those who truly deserve it never even saw that much in their entire careers. I think it boils down to somewhere along the way the message of empowerment got confused with entitlement. Instead of earning life's benefits, some think they can just reap them.

------Veronica

African American men are an endangered species. It is difficult to find those who are heterosexual, successful, spiritual, dedicated, and faithful.

------Kim

My overall perception of African American males- and really any male, for that matter-- is that they are more egocentric than females. This sometimes makes them appear dominant, self-centered, maybe even selfish and inconsiderate at times. They also appear protective, but it could be that often times it is driven by the whole ego, self-image thing. If they feel they possess or own a woman, they will protect her, but at the same time that same woman will come second in other instances.

-------Raven

Black males are rare. Strong black men are not in numbers. Many black males are weak in some areas but strong in some.

------Ashley

Most older African American males have my utmost respect simply because of their daily struggles and strength. Current young African American males truly concern me. Their morals and values seem to have disintegrated. Maybe it has a lot to do with the fact that parents of a lot of our current young African American males are so much younger. Children seem to be raising children. A lot of African American fathers have not accepted or have refused to accept their responsibilities. Respect does not seem to be valued. This includes respect for self, others, the community, etc.

-------*Shonda*

My husband was loving, kind, and a friend. He was a good provider and a churchgoing man.

------*Nancy*

I hate to make any generalizations about black men because my father is a black man, my uncles are black men, and my brothers are black men. Overall, the black men in my family are caring, respectful, responsible family men. On the other hand, the men I've been in relationships with have been dishonest, have failed to take responsibility, and were ultimately a big disappointment.

-------*Mia*

I believe African American males are caught up into societies' perceptions of them and they hear the negative so much they start to believe that's who they are, and they become just that.

------Dawn

GH Final Thoughts:

Brothers are taught to be strong, and for many showing weakness is not acceptable. A significant portion of a brother's persona is shaped by his previous experiences in life. His relationship with his parents or maybe the lack thereof, and the experiences he has had with the female population all have a lot to do with his actions and behavior in relationships.

As you can see, there are many opinions on brothers and their overall motives and desire in regard to relationships. I believe that when brothers enter into relationships, they do so with expectations, which they usually expect to be met. But often sisters feel that brothers fail to realize that many of their expectations are sometimes unrealistic, which could cause problems from the onset of the relationship. To be able to communicate what each person wants from the relationship and be honest enough to admit whether you can or cannot meet these goals is critical for the success of a relationship.

Chapter 7

Loving Too Many

Another sad reality is that brothers are often in numerous relationships at any given time. Each one of these relationships comes in different form and contains various meanings. A good relationship depends on how brothers feel about themselves as well as the women in their lives. There are also brothers whose behaviors are influenced by friends and male family members who may take great pleasure in degrading sisters with whom they have been in relationships with for many years. There are many different things that affect the way brothers feel about being in a committed relationship, and at the very top is their perception of sisters. How he views his partner and her role in the relationship will give a significant indication of the relationship's success. It is my hope that before brothers and sisters embark upon a relationship, they would first become true friends and companions. It is only through spending time getting to know one another that they can actually determine whether their relationship is built on love or infatuation. A person does not enter a relationship only because he/she loves someone, but rather because of how that person makes them feel.

Although some brothers may present this macho façade and engage in several relationships at one time, most actually want a loving and supportive sister to challenge and encourage them in a positive way. Of course, there are sisters who are willing to step up to the plate; as one sister surveyed revealed, "No matter what condition an African American male is in, she would and should be the backbone of the black man, to stand behind him and uplift him when bad times occur." After reading this, I was reminded of a radio show I was listening to when the host, who happened to be a brother, made the statement, "When are our African American men going to begin taking care of the sisters who take care of us regardless of what condition we are in?" With this said, it is obvious that sisters have often been willing to accept brothers regardless of their sometimes troubling conditions and have always been the glue that kept the African American family together.

In this quest of trying to understand our black brothers, we must certainly look at the other side of the equation in that there are huge stereotypes being reinforced by the media and by some sisters who have had negative experiences with brothers saying that African American males are no good. As a friend of mine so eloquently put it, "African American males have had a hard way to go in corporate America as well as in life in general. Therefore, what sisters have to realize is that sometimes you have brothers who may really want to do well, but society doesn't always allow them the opportunities to do as well as they could, but you have to be very supportive and encouraging." Therefore, in this journey to understand brothers, it is important for sisters to know that our forefathers were a strong and resilient group of men and have always had to possess strength and courage in the midst of darkness and uncertainty.

COMMENTS:

I worry about this trend among black men having many "baby mommas" and not financially caring for their children. These men are disrespectful to black women, disrespectful to themselves, and disrespectful of the children who never know their father because he's out running the streets. I worry about black men who have no real purpose in life. The prison system has taken many, but unfortunately, many of the ones who are walking among us have little direction for their present and their future. I fear that many black women, in their attempt to love and be loved, are making some extremely poor choices when it comes to the men that they are allowing into their lives. These women may feel good that they "have a man," but I feel sorry for them because when I look at many of them, I can see that they are anything but happy. I believe that the sadness that I see in their eyes is based on their knowledge that the male that they affectionately call "my man" is consistently disrespecting them by cheating on them, cursing them, hitting them, and financially exploiting them (oftentimes in front of their children). Because I am examining this from a spiritual/biblical perspective, I believe that it is primarily the responsibility of black men to "step up to the plate" in this regard.

------*Keisha*

To me, African American males are lazy and careless. Not all black males, but today a number of black males are in jail, dead, unemployed, or looking for some female to take care of them. That's why I say they are lazy. They are careless because of the way they are sleeping with all these women and not protecting themselves from AIDS.

------*Nicole*

53

Overall, my perception of the male species is not wholly negative, but there is some negativity, one being sleeping with too many women. But although there are some negative aspects of males, there are still a lot of positives, and I don't see the male species as a generality; there are still good males. And although there are some negatives, one should never be hopeless; change can always occur.

------*Anita*

I think it is hard for a large percentage of males to commit to be honest in relationships. I think they want women to believe they are committed to them, but are afraid to admit that they are in relationships with more than one woman. My perception of this comes from personal relationships, from hearing unfortunate stories from friends and coworkers, and from keeping up with current events. Male/female violence often makes the news. I think some men are habitual users. I also think some are addicted to sex and cannot control themselves.

------*Trisha*

I believe African American males are caught up into society's perceptions of them, and they hear the negative so much they start to believe that's who they are, and they become just that.

-------*Kim*

GH Final Thoughts:

Trisha really hit it on the head when she talks about males having a hard time committing to a relationship. I think that every sister knows of one, two, or maybe three friends who are going through some drama in their relationship. It is clear that a number of brothers are playing games, and sex is the prize. It is my opinion that women are giving brothers sex at such an alarming rate with little to no strings attached, that this could be why this sister feels that some men are habitual users and addicted to sex. I have heard it said that "sex is the only addiction that no one complains about." With this said, it may be a good time to stress the importance of being safe when engaging in sexual activities. I think it is important for sisters to understand that when you have unprotected sex with someone, you are literally having sex with everyone that person has had sex with, and this could be dangerous. I know some may be asking, what is she talking about? Well, unfortunately, we are living in a world where your sexual mistakes could kill you. Check out what Nicole had to say. Please forgive me, but I must refer back to Trisha's comments about males having a hard time when it comes to honesty in relationships because there is this great desire to get laid by as many women as possible. Whoever said that men will go to hell and back for sex came really close, and it is absolutely true.

During my research for this book New York was in an uproar over their governor, Eliot Spitzer's resignation after allegations surfaced about his having ties to a prostitution ring. It was reported that the governor spent $80,000 for these services. To add more gas to the fire, the Lieutenant Governor, David Paterson, slated to take Governor Spitzer's place, on the day of his inauguration revealed that he and his wife had had extra marital affairs. And in yet another sex scandal, Detroit's first black mayor, Kwame Kilpatrick, stepped down from his post amid allegations of his having an affair with his chief of staff. And there is the story of South Carolina's governor, Mark Sanford, going missing for several days with no one knowing his whereabouts. Upon returning, Governor Sanford admitted traveling to Argentina to be with his lover, leaving his wife and family alone over the Father's Day weekend. There seems to be a fascination about these sensational stories and the destruction that usually follows. The question that is being asked is how these men, who seemed to have it all, could risk everything for sex.

To men, sex is a necessity; it is a craving unlike any other craving that one can imagine. Men love sex, and the more they can get the better.

I must take this time to share a little secret with the sisters. It is important for women to realize the power that comes with the sex which they are so freely giving away. You have something that men want and desire but you must also understand that every other sister with breath in her body has the same ability to give sex as well. Power is only power when you control it, and I know that many will say that I am putting a little too much emphasis on this sex thing, but believe it or not, sex does have an element of power, but not sex alone.

Chapter 8

Single Parent, Doing It Alone

I am sure if you ask any mother what is the most challenging and important job she has ever had, she would probable say raising my child(ren). Children are indeed a blessing from God. It takes a lot of responsibility, sacrifice, patience, and love to raise good children. Sadly, many sisters have neglected to think of this when they decide to get pregnant without being in a committed relationship or marriage. Now I know that many sisters will say, "I was not trying to get pregnant; it just happened. Others have said, "The brother wanted me to have his baby." Believe it or not, I have also heard, "I thought it would make our relationship better."

There are some sisters who need to realize that a baby or babies will not under any circumstances make a brother marry her or stay in a relationship with her. If the relationship is not built on a strong foundation, then it is only a matter of time before he moves on and leaves her to raise her child or children alone as a single parent.

To be completely honest, there are many sisters who use pregnancy as a tool to entrap their lovers into a committed relationship. And when it backfires, they are often enraged, heartbroken, and bitter.

I really think that sisters need to stop being so naive and easy, allowing brothers to impregnate them, knowing that they are not going to commit to the relationship or that he may or may not provide for the child. It seems that some sisters are so desperate to have a brother in their life that they find it necessary to try to use an innocent child as glue to hold a relationship together. If you are in an unproductive relationship, be real with yourself. If the relationship is not compatible from the beginning, there is no way a child will keep it together.

Now I certainly understand that sometimes things happen and the result may be a baby, but the message I am trying to get out is please be careful by whom you have a child. This decision could affect the rest of your life as well as the life of your child. It is sisters who are often left to struggle to provide for their children and often have to give up their dreams and goals to take on this wonderful but tough job.

It was during a social gathering that a friend of mine and mother of two expressed that she had worked very hard to make her marriage work because she had seen her mother struggle trying to raise three children as a single parent, and this experience opened her eyes to just how tough a job raising children alone could be. She went on to state that she learned to compromise in order to keep her family together.

It has been proven that children who are reared in single-parent homes, usually by their mothers, do not fare as well emotionally, academically, and socially as children who are reared in a stable two-parent home. With that in mind, I do not believe that a sister is incapable of rearing her children on her own, because this arrangement is better than having her children in a home filled with turmoil. I myself am a product of a single-parent home, but there were many wonderful people who played a tremendous role in my upbringing and who showered me with love and encouragement. Although my father did not live with me, he always encouraged me to strive for something better.

But I am still disturbed by this trend of sisters rearing children without a positive father figure in the lives of their children. As someone who advocates for children and study their development; research reveals that black boys have a harder road to travel than their Caucasian counterparts. According to some statistics, in most large cities the dropout rate of African American males is about 50 percent and many sociologists equate this to being raised in an environment without the presence of a positive male role model. In 1920, ninety percent of African American youths had their father present. In 1960, it was eighty percent, presently; it is only thirty- two percent. Therefore, it is very important to the well-being of our young males that they are able to see brothers in a positive and productive light.

Although I believe it is ideal to have a two-parent home for children, I strongly believe that the most important thing that one can give a child is love, a good education, and a strong sense of self.

COMMENTS:

There is so much to be said about this so important issue of single parent households. We would really have to go to the root of a lot of issues, starting with our children raising themselves, because that single mother is out working trying to provide for her child, while the child is home alone allowing television and the world to raise him/her. Our children don't know the value of family, because they didn't grow up in one; therefore, when they are grown and get married, they don't know what a family is. They don't know what it means to be a husband, a provider, and a backbone for the family. Our black women need to stop allowing our black brothers to get them pregnant, knowing that they are not going to commit to the relationship and be a provider for them. Our black women appear to be hard up for a man, and they settle for any man and marry him. Only two months down the line, they will be in divorce court. Then the cycle starts again, another single mother raising her child, alone!

------*Keisha*

I think that homes headed by single parents have a potential to have a positive or negative effect, depending on the strength of those parents and what they teach or instill in their children.

------*Kim*

I feel as though children need a mother and a father in their lives. Children need to see how adults interact with each other in life. I also understand the reasoning why there are so many households that are being dominated by single mothers. Children need to see men in a positive light. Little boys need to learn how to be a man and what exactly that means and what it takes to be a man. Little girls need to see how a man should treat a woman so that when they grow up they will find a man who will treat them with respect.

------*Jessica*

GH Final Thoughts:

Through research I discovered that black women have always been more likely to give birth outside marriage, although recently the gap has narrowed as the out-of-wedlock birthrate for whites has increased, while it has slightly fallen for black women. I was also surprised to learn that having children outside of marriage is associated with a lower likelihood that a sister will ever marry, which could shed some light on why there is such a large number of African American women who are unmarried and raising children alone.

Of all major demographic groups, African American single mothers and their children are the worst off economically. I read that some low-income mothers believe that they are better off without a partner in their home. It is my assumption that these mothers are doing what they need to do in order to keep benefits they may be receiving from the state. Whatever the reasons may be, there is a large number of African American children being raised in single-parent homes, often with no positive male role model in their lives. As Jessica expressed, children need to have the presence of both their parents in their home to really get a clear knowledge of the values and morals that should exist within a family structure, but if there is no positive male role model, then it is the job of the parent who is present to provide their children with the guidance and nurturing needed to become well-rounded individuals. Remember you are the example for your children when it comes to nurturing and love.

Chapter 9

Communication

Good communication is the key to intimacy and passion in a loving, committed relationship. Communication is not simply expressing views. It is the method by which individuals express feelings, desires, and needs. One of the main reasons for the high divorce rate today, especially among African Americans, is the inability of brothers and sisters to truly communicate with each other.

I believe that some brothers and sisters are afraid to let their lovers know their exact emotions. Many African Americans are reluctant to openly explore their deepest hopes, painful past, hidden resentments, or lack of self-confidence out of fear that they will be looked upon as being weak. On more than one occasion, I have heard friends and associates reveal that they would never tell a partner they love them because if they expressed their love, the partner might think he/she had the upper hand. There seems to be a fear that letting a lover know them will be humiliating or will lead them to feel inferior. This type of behavior makes creating and sustaining a great love relationship difficult, if not impossible.

Intimacy for brothers and sisters can be frightening. But it is through this intimacy that a relationship can blossom into a new and exhilarating world of happiness, while fear of giving of ourselves can lead to pain and suffering. The process of developing a positive relationship requires the ability to establish a genuine friendship with the person with whom you are interested in cultivating a relationship with, and the only way that this is achieved is through communication. This is what intimacy is- the ability to share feelings and develop trust.

But studies have shown that sisters complain that brothers are irresponsible, not trustworthy, and can't make a commitment, while brothers counter that sisters are demanding, difficult, and very materialistic. So the question remains, "How can someone develop a long-term intimate involvement with someone whom they are not willing to trust?" The answer lies in both sisters and brothers being able to clear their minds of the negative stereotypes about each other. Not all brothers are dogs, trifling, or unwilling to commit. Nor are all sisters only interested in money or material things. With this said, the million dollar question is, "What needs to be done to make brothers and sisters communicate the language of love to each other?"

In order for this to occur, brothers must openly communicate with sisters, making themselves available to their partner by using clear and kind words, loving thoughts and gentle, soft touches. They both must express their feelings verbally and allow their companion to do the same. Brothers and sisters must actively listen and attempt to understand each other's thoughts and feelings, no matter how sentimental, difficult, or uncomfortable they may seem. Brothers must respect and acknowledge sisters, and recognize them as individuals with their own minds. Brothers and sisters need to be allowed to express their own thoughts in their own way, without the fear of being judged. It is only after achieving this acceptance of each other that two people can explore all the good and bad of the other's inner self. Getting to know and be known by your partner is exciting and emotionally enriching. The freedom of expression is the key to communicating with each other, even in tough times.

Brothers often experience few intimate moments and poor communication due often to their upbringing and pressures of everyday life. Many of the social difficulties that young brothers endured during their childhood often stem from living in homes with major money issues, continual conflict among adults within their home, and sometimes lack of expressions of love from their parents and other adults. What begins to happen is that they start emulating the behavior of the people around them and thus experience the same painful series of events that occurred in their childhood.

Although communication can be difficult regardless of race or gender, the African American families seem to be more affected by the lack of positive communication skills. This may be the effect of young brothers having been told that they are weak if they communicate their feelings. Many of these brothers feel that self-protection and living up to a "bad boy" image is more important than self-love and emotional growth.

Just as sisters need to take a hard look within themselves to evaluate who they really are, brothers need to do the same. It is wise that brothers examine what makes them think and communicate the way they do and what are their hot-button issues. Both brothers and sisters need to identify what they have to offer to a relationship, what makes them unique and different, and not just their sexual performance. They must take full responsibility for their lives and the direction they want their lives to go. It is imperative that brothers develop a sense of what a good relationship looks like and how to discipline themselves to become accommodating and emotionally available to their partners by expressing their feelings. So what is making me curious is:

What happens when two people within a committed relationship stop talking, listening, and becoming intimate with each other?

The fact is when couples stop displaying affection toward each other, often that love connection that originally sealed the relationship begins to erode, which may cause the lines of communication to close.

Maintaining joy and passion within a relationship is the lifeline of a healthy and happy union. This usually happens when brothers and sisters are connected to each other and feel that they are respected, heard, and understood. But I am sure there are sisters who want to know:

Do I have to tell everything?

Although openness through communication is essential to personal growth and intimacy, it certainly needs to be undertaken carefully. Total openness can impose an unrealistic standard upon relationships. To say that brothers and sisters should keep no secrets from one another and that complete honesty is always the best policy fails to recognize the human need for some privacy. For example, if you don't feel comfortable sharing the sexual details of a past relationship, there is no reason to feel as though you must, as long as you have practiced safe sex and all your past relationships are a thing of the past. Openness does not mean that you have to tell your partner every single detail. I am sure that everyone can recall at least one situation when information that you communicated to your partner about something that happened in a past relationship has been used against you in your current and present relationship and this disclosure has created conflict and chaos about something that has absolutely nothing to do with the person you are with. Some things are really better left unspoken.

COMMENTS:

There has always been a breakdown between men and women in general. I am currently reading a book entitled "Men Are from Mars, Women from Venus" which has highlighted some very interesting facts. Until we take the time to understand the nature of the two specimens, the communication breakdown will always exist. It's like going to a foreign country (planet) and not being able to speak the language or understand the culture. Until couples take the time to learn those different aspects, only then will they be able to understand and communicate.

------*Tasha*

There are communication problems within relationships, but these problems don't just exist between African American males and females, but between the males and females of all cultures. In the African American community, this communication breakdown just exists to a larger degree, and African American males are more reluctant to get counseling or to accept that there is anything amiss. So if one feels that nothing is wrong, then one feels that there is nothing to mend.

------*Anita*

God, yes, there is a breakdown. More listening should be done instead of talking for African American males and females. Communication should be a two-way interaction.

------*Jada*

The problem that we have is that we misinterpret the messages we get from one another.

------*Trisha*

I think that advantages and disadvantages are different for African American males and females, and as a result these differences sometimes blur the lines of communication between African American males and females.

------*Ashley*

I do believe many of us (male/female) should make improvements in how we communicate with one another. I think respect is an essential element.

------*Brenda*

There is a breakdown in communication, but not specifically between African American males and females. There appears to be a breakdown in communication throughout the human race.

------*Dana*

There are some occasional struggles in my relationship, but we keep the lines of communication open. We don't argue or fight, we try to "let each other off the hook" by communicating our needs or dislikes.

------*Brianna*

I definitely think there is a breakdown in communication but not only between African-American males and females but with all males and females. No matter what the color or culture... If your man is watching a sporting event... it is not the time to try to have a heart-to-heart-talk with him! :) I think that is universal. I do think that specifically between African-American males and females we have a more difficult time communicating with each other because there is so much confusion with our own identities. Not biracial identities confusion, but who we are as individuals. How well do we know ourselves, are we happy and accepting of that. If we either don't really know what we want for and out of ourselves, how can we know what we want for and from someone else? If we don't know, then it is impossible for them to know; therefore, you have a failed relationship. Once we have an idea of who we are (and it changes), then we know what we want, what we will and will not accept or settle for (and that too changes) then, we can bring someone else into that precious space of ours. We must let them know up front so they can decide if they can adapt their "program" to yours and if you both can make compromises to your individual plan, not to yourselves, and make one plan that is acceptable to both of you. When this is working; there is nothing more beautiful than BLACK LOVE! (That's why we swoon for President and First Lady Obama)

------*Veronica*

I believe the breakdown in communication between African American males and African American females is brought about because of underlying family issues, morals, and values.

------*Dawn*

GH Final Thoughts:

I think it is fair to say that the overall perception of these sisters is that there are problems in the area of communication not just in the African American community but, as Anita and Dana stated, between males and females of all cultures. While I was teaching a lesson on the importance of communication to a group of parents, out of the blue, a young lady asked me a somewhat surprising question. She wanted to know how I had fallen in love with my husband. Although I found it a strange question, I realized that as part of our activities and discussions from the lessons that it was obvious to the ladies that communication was a high priority within my marriage, and I truly believe it is at the core of every relationship formed; be it with your children, partner, parents, etc., language is critical. I went on to explain to her that I had fallen in love with my husband through our ability to have wonderful conversations. I revealed to her how we would go out to dinner and would sit and talk for hours. It was so refreshing to be able to openly express my dreams and desires to someone and have him understand and support me and know that I would do the same for him. I was well aware that in order to create and sustain long-lasting love, we needed to be able to communicate what we wanted early in our relationship and to continue this process as time went on. One thing that I had learned early in my life was that individuals do not fall in love through sexual experiences, but that people fall in love through the art of communication. Communication is the key to any relationship. It is the method by which individuals get to know each other.

Chapter 10

New Love and Loving It

When we fall in love, it is with a person that we think we know. In the beginning of relationships, individuals are always putting their best foot forward. You want to look your best; you are very careful when it comes to your conversation. The newness is still there and the mission at this point is often to explore the most positive aspects of our mate. There seems to be a magic in the air when you are together. Usually, at this point each person begins feeling accepted, cared for, and loved. There is a new rush of excitement and energy which can be phenomenal. The relationship is filled with laughter, playfulness, exhilarating sex, and passion. God, this love feels so good! But as time goes on, couples become comfortable with each other, and the steamy energy often goes flat. We realize that our partners are not perfect and have flaws just as we do. And that intensive connection seems somehow to get lost in time. It was at a group meeting that a classmate talked about being recently divorced after 17 years of marriage and wanting to experience new love again. She talked about wanting to go on dates, share ice cream and holding hands because so much of that had been absent in the 17 years of her marriage. While listening to this, I began wondering why these small gestures had to disappear and at what point in the relationship had they begun leaving.

COMMENTS:

My love is a breath of freshness. It happened when I thought it had simply looked over me. It happened when I thought that God forgot about sending me that special love just for me. But one thing for sure, it couldn't have happened soon enough nor with a more genuine and sincere individual. Experiencing this love makes me smile when I don't even realize I'm smiling and knowing that those smiles come from thoughts of him. Experiencing this love tames my heart to be more open, forgiving, understanding and joyous. Experiencing new love gives me the opportunity to know that this world no longer tackles me alone but us together as one confronting any obstacles that we may face. I am on cloud nine with my new LOVE!!!

------*Monique*

This is a great love that makes me feel that I am on top of the world. The feeling of having someone to love and care about you is incredible!!!

------*Tracy*

Love is putting God first and putting egos aside. Open and effective communication, self-love, and independence will eliminate the neediness or the search for the opposite sex to fulfill any voids. If these things are involved, then love should be able to stay new and last no matter what.

------*Brianna*

GH Final Thoughts:

In my opinion, love is something that everyone wants to experience, but not everyone finds it. After reading these statements, it really took me back to the beginning of my relationship with my husband. The joy and excitement of having someone to share your daily activities and common interests is a great delight. Love is the greatest high!! I can remember it like it was yesterday but after 8 years of marriage and 12 years of being together, I realize that the most important factor in our relationship was the commitment that we shared with each other to make our marriage work, despite our imperfections. When people fall in love they discover a wide open channel of expression with each other. Inevitably, the sparks may start to fade and the day-to-day struggles of real life situations start to creep in. It is at this point that you must remind yourself of what made you come together in the beginning. Love is not an easy task; it takes continuous work. The sparks don't have to fade, but you must realize that whatever you did to capture a person's love is the same thing, plus a little more is needed to keep it. I was told by someone that love is an uncontrollable emotion and that the heart has its own plan. The heart wants what it wants and there is often nothing that you can do about it.

Chapter 11

Advice for the Brothers

I thought it might be a good idea to allow sisters to give brothers some advice, given the fact that brothers are the best at saying what a sister needs to do. There is no need for me to go any further; I will let the sisters state their cases.

COMMENTS:

Brothers need to have pride about themselves and to be mature. What is important is what is in your head and not the head in your pants. They need to respect themselves as well as females, to realize that they are somebody and deserving of everything this world has to offer. Go out and get it with education and hard work. Teach your children to have values and to have children with one woman, and not have them all over the place and not taking care of them.

------*Rena*

I would tell brothers that it's okay to show their sensitive side to their wives or girlfriends. That's important in relationships.

------*Core*

Respect your African American sisters even when they don't deserve it. Lean and depend on good values and morals. Accept your responsibilities and consequences for your actions. Respect yourself above all others; and others will follow. Always lead by example. Don't be miserable simply because of a relationship of "convenience."

------*Shonda*

Be faithful and grateful. Learn to be satisfied; the grass is not always greener on the other side.

------*Cindy*

Know who you are. Are you a leader or a follower? Know the type of woman you want and need; there may be a difference between the two. Understand that a relationship is about compromise and no longer about "this is how I do it" but how is it best for us. If you meet an independent woman, don't dismiss her as not wanting you with not needing you; it could become a beautiful relationship. Don't allow things to define you but your heart and actions. Love God, yourself, and your Black Woman! You know we aren't easily broken and are "Ride or Die" for the right one and unfortunately sometimes for the wrong one(s)!

------*Veronica*

Advice for African American males would be to learn how to be men, open the door for a lady when she is entering or exiting a building, learn to pay attention to the little things in life, strive to be better, don't succumb to the societal statistics of African American males, pull your pants up, stop with the tattoos, and quit with the gold/ platinum teeth.

------*Dawn*

Be honest. Even if it hurts the person who wants more than you are ready to give. If you are not ready for a monogamous relationship, say it early in the relationship. Do not marry unless you are committed.

------*Jessica*

Learn to love GOD and yourself, and if you want REAL LOVE, give REAL LOVE. You can't get what you don't give.

------*Shelia*

GH Final Thoughts:

My primary goal here is to shed a little light on what sisters want brothers to know. Sisters are asking for honesty, faithfulness, sensitivity, and self-respect as well as respect for them. I have always said you cannot respect someone else if you don't have respect for yourself. I love the point that Rena is making regarding brothers understanding that they are somebody and deserving of everything this world has to offer. She goes on to talk about getting an education and the importance of hard work, which is at the cornerstone of what America was built on.

I also want brothers to know that there are a number of sisters who understand their struggles, and as an African American woman, I am certainly aware of the institutional racism that exists within our society and would like for other sisters to realize this as well. But for the sisters that don't, let me fill you in on something. There are brothers who possess the knowledge and skills needed to succeed in today's workplace, but some may have taken on a defeated attitude while maneuvering through this sometimes marginalized system. Some sisters may look down on the position of some brothers without a true appreciation of their situation in life or the various social and economic pressures they face. My advice to brothers is keep your head high, equip yourself with an education or vocational trade, stay within the law, network with positive individuals, set goals, and aggressively pursue your dreams.

Chapter 12

Sisters on Sisterhood

There is something about the bond of sisterhood that can be unlike any other bond one might experience. This connection is filled with many joys, pains, laughter, celebrations, sorrow, tears, and shared experiences. Webster defines friend as someone who is personally well-known by oneself and for whom one holds warm regards. To me friendship is a very important role, one which I have tried to take very seriously. My husband always said that you will have many acquaintances and associates in your lifetime, but when it comes to real friends you will find that number will be few.

Although, just like anyone else, I have sometimes fallen short in regard to friends, I realize that all friendships go through ups and downs, and mine are no exception. Some friendships are able to stand the test of time, blossom, and grow as each sister embraces life's successes and failures. But this bond, this connection, has an odd way of bringing our differences into view. Sometimes these differences have caused some women to fight, compete, compare, and become resentful of each other. These feelings, if not controlled, could eventually lead to jealousy. Jealousy is a mental attitude which is characterized by serious resentment of another person's accomplishments, attractiveness, recognition, possessions, or by anger toward someone because of qualities or some advantages they may possess.

Many sisters may not want to believe that this could be a reality of our existence; the fact is that there does seem to be a disconnection between sisters and even among women in general. A few years ago, while waiting in an airport, I overheard a group of sisters traveling together in conversation. One lady made a statement that really captured my attention; she said women can sometimes be petty and cold. This really made me think about the way that sisters viewed each other and the role that competition and other petty behaviors play in our lives and just how society has contributed to this mind-set.

It is obvious that we live in a world that idealizes material wealth, and what this seems to have created is a society of people that are fixated on who has what. Given this information, it is my hope that sisters understand that there will always be women who have more than you. It could be a better grade of hair, a higher paying job, a bigger house, a loving and caring boyfriend or husband, a finer car, a better body, and the list could go on and on. This kind of animosity, which often exists, is absolutely pointless, because no one gains when sisters compete with each other.

As a sister myself, I have felt sometimes the coldness of fellow sisters for whatever reason, but I have refused to allow the negative behavior of others to deter my positive attitude toward other sisters whom I encounter. I have always considered myself to be a "people" person and feel that I can relate to almost any woman, but I do realize that not all sisters can relate to each other. It is my opinion that the mass media, through television and movies, have put more people in direct competition with each other - especially women. With this said, it is no secret that, in addition to our society idealizing material wealth, there is also a fascination with beauty and attractiveness, which leads me to this question:

Has society's obsession with beauty affected the relationships of women?

There is an assumption in our society that attractive people are more fulfilled, popular, and happy. Although studies do show that there is some truth to this, what has been found is that attractive people as young children often received more attention from family members, and that helped them develop positive characteristics. It is also assumed that attractive women also have more choices in romantic partners, which may or may not lead to more power in relationships which could result in marrying brothers with higher financial stability, which in turn could result in improving their quality of life.

It has been said that women are judged more on attractiveness and men more on financial status when it comes to finding a mate. Research shows that women are usually jealous of more attractive women which may shed some light on the tension that seems to sometimes exist within the sisterhood. It was evident from my studies while in gradate school that there is a ratio imbalance within the African American race in regard to men and women. Sisters greatly outnumber brothers due to many factors such as the high incarceration and mortality rates among African American males, as well as the growing number of homosexuals just to name a few. With this said, competition is high among sisters given the fact that most are bidding for the affection of the rare suitable brothers available. Therefore, one can see how a certain amount of resentment and hostility might have a way of creeping into a friendship or potential friendship when one person feels that she may not possess certain qualities that could be looked upon within our society as desirable.

Sexual attraction usually begins at the level of physical appearance; this includes many features such as hair, skin tone, body size, or figure. Men are creatures of eye-sight and are often drawn to women who are pleasing to the eye, but this is not to say that every brother is out making his selection in regard to a sister based solely on her level of physical attractiveness. But there is obviously an obsession with beauty within our society, and men seem to value attractiveness more than women. For some brothers, there is an awareness that the way that others judge them often depends on the attractiveness of the woman he has on his arm. This is the sad reality of the world in which we live, and it is my opinion this could be one of the reasons why some sisters may not be willing to embrace other sisters because of what that sister has or how she looks, which is pathetic to say the least. I think it would be fair to ask:

What is the issue, and how can we make things better?

I think that the real issue is that women don't really trust each other, which can open the door for feelings of uncertainty about each other. Let me say that real friendship or sisterhood can only exist when respect and trust is present. Friendship is always a two-way street where each person looks out for the best interest of the other, supporting and encouraging each other's successes. As women, we each need to make a conscious effort to uplift our friends regardless of their accomplishments or lack of accomplishments, recognition, attractiveness, or possessions. I am completely aware of the fact that some attractive and accomplished sisters sometimes seem to have this superiority complex and attitude, but not all sisters are like this, and many are hurt at the idea that others view them this way. The only person that you need to compete against is yourself. Strive to be the best that you can be for you, and realize that competing against other women to prove yourself better can be emotionally and psychologically draining.

COMMENTS:

The black women I know are strong, confident, educated, and loving Christian women. My 90-year-old grandmother, the matriarch of our family, possesses all of these qualities and more. My grandmother and my mother are truly remarkable women. On the other hand, I believe many black women tend to sell themselves short, placing their children, men, careers, etc., before their own personal goals and desires. We should require a happy medium.

------*Tonya*

My overall perception of African American females is: they are competitive (sometimes to a fault) for good men, love, affection, employment, etc.

------*Kim*

African American females are lowering their standards because of the African American males and their outlook on life. Sisters are very strong and ambitious in being independent and successful in life. However, many tend to take those things for granted and use it as a negative rather than a positive.

------*Dawn*

My perception of African American females is that they are more demanding and sometimes can be more forceful than they need to be, especially when dealing with a mate or spouse.

------*Yolanda*

First of all, African American females are beautiful. Older generations are so strong, yet these older African American females are the last of a dying "breed." Many younger African American females are often too aggressive. Respect is not given; respect is earned. Younger African American females should enjoy their childhood. They should not try to experience adult life during their precious childhood. Young African American females want to do too much too fast.

-------*Shonda*

African American females possess some negative aspects. The self-respect, need for respect from their men, and hard work ethics of bygone days are missing. By the same token, hope still exists for change.

------*Shelia*

GH Final Thoughts:

It is wonderful to see sisters like Tonya and Shonda talk about the African American women they know who are strong, confident, educated, and beautiful. This is a direct contrast to the description that society has sometimes placed on us, like aggressive, angry, and confrontational, to name a few. Although I have encountered people of the other gender and other races that also fit these same descriptions, but their behaviors usually come with an explanation clarifying the reasons behind their actions.

I am sure that you have heard, "A friend who leads is a friend indeed," which could give some insight on the essence of real sisterhood. Having a friend with whom to share the good and not so good of life can be priceless. A Harvard Medical School study found that the more friends a woman has, the less likely are her chances of developing physical impairment as she ages. Although I am aware that there are many great benefits to having these wonderful connections with sisters, friendships can be complicated and occasionally complex, especially when women begin going through different stages in their life, like marriage, divorce, parenting, and different career paths which sometimes could cause people to drift apart. It is at this time that one should evaluate to see just how important that relationship is and come up with creative ways to keep the friendship alive. There is nothing better than the bond between loving and caring friends.

Chapter 13

Marriage Within the African American Community

There is no doubt that the patterns of marriage in the United States have changed dramatically in recent decades, as reflected by trends toward older ages at first marriage, lower marriage rates, higher rates of divorce and separation, and a greater prevalence of female- headed families, as mentioned in a previous chapter. Although these trends are pervasive, they are more pronounced among African Americans. While I was in graduate school, my studies showed that compared to whites, black Americans, especially sisters, tend to separate and divorce earlier in their marriages and are less likely to remarry. I was also surprised to discover that African Americans have the lowest marriage rate of any racial group in the United States. In 2001, according to the U.S. Census, 43.3 percent of African American men and 41.9 percent of African American women had never been married, in contrast to 29 percent and 21.8 percent respectively for whites (U.S. Census, 2001). I must say I was taken aback when I came across this information, but I was not really surprised because in just observing my circle of friends and family, there weren't that many places to look and see successful marriages within the African American community. What I found, and we must keep it real, was that there are a large number of brothers who are incarcerated, the mortality rate among young brothers is extremely high, they are often underemployed, and there is a group of brothers who are not interested in gaining employment and who are looking for a sister to take care of them. This is unfortunate because it could make it harder for those sisters who are trying to find a good brother with whom to cultivate a relationship. Now I am not saying that it is impossible to find that special person, but what I am saying is that sisters have to be very careful when selecting a mate.

One sister expressed on her survey form that, "Marriage is not easy and literally requires the death of your own motives." She went on to reveal, "You cannot manipulate or demand your own way in a marriage, and you must be willing to compromise even when it doesn't line up with your way. As African American women, many of us are raised to be independent and not to depend on a man." She goes on to say that this makes it hard for sisters to submit to brothers because submission and independence work against each other. It is her opinion that a relationship with the Lord is the only way to a successful marriage because God teaches us how to love. The words of this sister seemed to ignite something within my spirit. She continued by saying that a majority of people marry for the wrong reasons, like money or just to be able to say they have a husband or wife. "Let God bless you with your husband or wife and include him or her in all your decisions, and you will have a better marriage. Marry someone who knows, believes, and trusts in God, because unless a couple put Him first, everything will crumble." This sister really knows the benefits of having God in a marriage.

Many sisters have suffered emotional and psychological hardships in their marriage. It is really difficult to say just what some of the reasons for their suffering are, but it is my guess that often they have rushed into marriage with partners whom they have not taken the opportunity to get to know. It was during a meeting that a lady who had been twice divorced revealed to the group that the main problem and/or issues with her two failed marriages was the fact that she had not taken enough time to get to know either of her husbands. She went on to say that they were not bad people. "I have nothing bad to say about them; we get along wonderfully now, but neither was the man for me." She later explained that her mother had warned her that she was moving too fast, but she had not listened. Sometimes we are so wrapped up in the moment and the idea of having a husband that we close our eyes to clues that this marriage might not work.

COMMENTS:

"I got married too soon and for all the wrong reasons."

------*Nancy*

I married someone from another background, brought up differently, and it did not work out. We were constantly pulling against each other. I liked to read, and he wanted to play video games.

------*Core*

My marriage is better than I thought it would be. My husband is my best friend. He's my provider and my lover. He's a great father to my children; even though they're not his, he treats them like they are.

------*Terri*

Marriage being successful or not depends on the two people who made the vows in the first place. Marriage doesn't change you; it only brings out the person you really are, good or bad.

-------*Letha*

Marriage is a commitment and dedication. If both parties, not one, are not willing to make a commitment to themselves and their spouse, it can't and won't work.

------*Constance*

I believe that a good marriage can improve the quality of one's life. On the other hand, a bad marriage can take away from the quality of one's life. That being said, I do believe that good marriages can lead to deeper and more satisfying romantic relationships, especially when both partners are committed to making the marriage work and making their spouse happy. However, a bad marriage can leave a person feeling "sour" about marriage, lead to poor health, and "high conflict" relationships (or a pattern of "high conflict" relationships). But I feel that good, strong, stable marriages are the best for individuals, couples, and their children.

------*Keya*

GH Final Thoughts:

Whoever said marriages are complicated was not joking! The state of marriages and/or relationships between brothers and sisters can be tempestuous at times, and research shows that African Americans are less likely to marry, to stay married, or to remarry after their marriage has ended than any other ethnic group. But as one sister I surveyed stated, "African American families have some of the same obstacles that other ethnic groups have with marriage." She went on to express that "Marriage is difficult no matter what color you are." Another sister put it best of all "Marriage is a commitment and dedication; if both parties, not one, are not willing to make a commitment to themselves and their spouse, it can't and won't work."

One major point I would like to project to sisters is that, other than your parents, no one in the world will have a greater impact on your life than the man you become involved with. This decision alone could be your greatest dream or your worst nightmare, and this is why it is so very important that sisters are selective when it comes to finding a soul mate, because marriage is the ultimate commitment and certainly should not be taken lightly.

As mentioned in previous chapters, I have administered surveys, conducted focus groups and interviews to gain a better insight on sister's perceptions on marriages, relationships, and just how they felt about brothers and each other. As you can imagine, the data was very revealing and surprising.

The survey form requested the following information:

1. **What is your age range?**
In response to the question, 15 percent of the respondents were 18 to 25 years, 43 percent were 26 to 35 years, 17 percent were 36 to 45 years, 13 percent were 46 to 55 years, 12 percent were 56 years and older.

2. **What is your current status?**
In response to the question, 37 percent were single (never married), 36 percent indicated married, 17 percent indicated divorced, 3 percent were widowed, 5 percent indicated married/separated, 2 percent indicated cohabitation (living with someone).

3. **What is your education level?**
In response to the question, 1 percent of the respondents had less than a high school diploma, 16 percent were high school graduates/GED, 39 percent were college graduates, 20 percent indicated having advanced degrees, 23 percent indicated some college.

4. **What is the education level of your spouse/partner?**
In response to the question, 2 percent of the respondents had less than a high school diploma, 17 percent were high school graduates/GED, 14 percent were college graduates, 8 percent indicated advanced degrees, 17 percent indicated some college, 42 percent indicated not applicable.

5. **If married, is this your:**
In response to the question, 36 percent of the respondents indicated that this was their first marriage, 5

percent indicated second marriage, 3 percent indicated third marriage, 56 percent indicated not applicable.

6. **What is your religious affiliation?**
In response to the question, 7 percent of the respondents said they were Catholic, 60 percent were Baptist, 8 percent were Methodist, 7 percent were Protestant, 2 percent had no affiliation.

7. **At what age did you get married?**
In response to the question, 31 percent of the respondents were married between 18 to 25 years, 24 percent were married between 26 to 35 years, 2 percent between 36 to 45 years, 7 percent between 46 to 55 years, 0 percent were 56 and over, 41 percent indicated not applicable.

8. **How often do you attend religious services?**
In response to the question, 27 percent of the respondents attend services more than once a week, 43 percent about once a week, 16 percent at least once a month, 7 percent at least twice a year, 3 percent never.

9. **Would you say that you are:**
In response to the question, 36 percent of the respondents were very religious, 53 percent somewhat religious, 3 percent not very religious, 5 percent not religious at all.

10. **Is your income level:**
In response to the question, 16 percent higher than your spouse/partner, 34 percent lower than your

spouse/partner, 4 percent about the same, 44 percent were not applicable.

11. Do you think marriage improves the quality of your life?

In response to the question, 65 percent of the respondents responded yes, 25 percent responded no, 9 percent had no response.

12. Would you be open to marrying someone of another race/ethnicity?

In response to the question, 55 percent of the respondents responded yes, they were open to marrying someone of another race, 32 percent responded no, and 11 percent did not respond to this question.

13. Did you feel pressure to marry after the marriage of friends, family, etc...?

In response to the question, 10 percent of the respondents responded yes, they did feel pressure to marry after the marriage of friends or family, 68 percent responded no, and 21 percent did not respond to this question.

14. If your marriage ends, would you remarry?

In response to the question, 27 percent of the respondents responded yes, if their marriage ended they would remarry, 17 percent responded no, 29 percent responded don't know, 26 percent responded not applicable.

15. **Is your marriage what you thought it would be?**

In response to the question, 21 percent of the respondents responded yes that their marriage was what they thought it would be, 28 percent responded no, 49 percent responded not applicable, 1 percent gave no response.

16. **A large percentage of African American households are headed by single females. Do you believe that this has a positive or negative effect on the African American community as a whole?**

In response to the question, 17 percent of the respondents indicated that they believed that households headed by single females had a positive effect on the African American community as a whole, 61 percent responded it had a negative effect, and 17 percent responded that it had no effect.

17. **The federal government has proposed legislation to develop a program to offer financial consideration to couples receiving public assistance (welfare) to marry. Do you believe this will have a positive or negative effect on couples and their decision to marry or not?**

In response to the question, 28 percent of the respondents indicated that offering financial consideration to couples receiving public assistance to marry would have a positive effect on their decision, 46 percent responded that it would have a negative effect, 19 percent responded no effect, and 5 percent did not respond to this question.

18. Given the sometimes troubled conditions of African American males, do you believe that these conditions affect your desire to commit to marriage?

In response to the question, 52 percent of the respondents indicated yes, that the sometimes troubled conditions of African American males did affect their desire to commit to marriage, and 42 percent responded that these conditions had no effect on their desire to marry.

19. With the country's divorce rates at an all time high and the continuing issue of single-parent-headed households moving in an upward trend, what institution should offer assistance or programs to improve the status of marriages in the African American community?

In response to the question, 21 percent of the respondents responded government should offer assistance or programs to improve the status of marriages in the African American community, 50 percent responded that the churches should provide assistance or programs to improve the status of marriage, 9 percent responded private sector (employer-based programs), and14 percent responded there should be two or more programs to provide assistance.

References

Besharov, D. J., & West, A. (2001). African American Marriage Patterns. Hoover Press: Thernstrom. 95.

Bloomfield, H., Vettese, S., & Kory, R. (1989). Life Mates: The Love Fitness Program For A Lasting Relationship. New York: Penguin Books Canada Limited.

Cherlin, A. J. (1992). Marriage, Divorce, Remarriage. Massachusetts: Harvard University Press.

Cornish, G. R. (1998). 10 Bad Choices That Ruin Black Women Lives. New York: Three River Press.

Guttentage, M., Secord, P. F. (1983). *Too many women: The sex ratio question*

Beverly Hill. Sage Publications.

Jackson, J. J. (1971). But where are all the men? *Black Scholar,* 3, 30-41.

Lichter, D. T., Graefe, D. R., & Brown, J. B., (2003). Is Marriage a Panacea? Union Formation Among Economically-Disadvantaged Unwed Mothers. *Social Problems,* 50, 60-86.

Russell, K., Wilson, M., & Hall, R. (1992). The Color Complex The Politics of Skin Color Among African Americans. New York: Harcourt Brace Jovanovich.

Smith, G. E. (2000). More Than Sex Reinventing The Black Male Image. New York: Kensington Publishing Corp.

The Influence of Higher Education on Black Marriage. (2003). *The Journal of Blacks in Higher Education,* 34-36.

Tucker, M. B., & Mitchell-Kernan, C. (Eds) (1995). *The Decline in Marriage Among African Americans: Causes, Consequences, and Policy Implications.* New York: Sage Russell Foundation.

Wilson, W. J., & Neckerman, K. M. (1987). Poverty and Family Structure: The widening gap between evidence and public policy issues. In W. J. Wilson, *The Truly Disadvantaged* (pp 232-259). Chicago: University of Chicago Press.

www.ingramcontent.com/pod-product-compliance
Lightning Source LLC
Chambersburg PA
CBHW071209280526
45787CB00002B/614